WHEEL, CAMEL, FISH, and PLOW YOGA for YOU

WHEEL, CAMEL, FISH, and PLOW YOGA for YOU

by Rachel Carr

photographs by Edward Kimball

Prentice-Hall, Inc.
Englewood Cliffs, New Jersey

The following photographs are courtesy of Educational Activities
who have produced my record album, *Yoga for Young People*:

Kin Chung Chang, page 41;
Felicia Davis, page 40;
Earl Jarrett, page 42;
Mark Levine, page 49;
Shari Traister, pages 54 and 55.

Frontispiece photo: Eva Denes and Earl Jarrett.

Design by Ronnie Ann Herman
Line drawings by Marjorie Thier

Prentice-Hall International, Inc., London
Prentice-Hall of Australia, Pty. Ltd., North Sydney
Prentice-Hall of Canada, Ltd., Toronto
Prentice-Hall of India Private Ltd., New Delhi
Prentice-Hall of Japan, Inc., Tokyo
Prentice-Hall of Southeast Asia Pte. Ltd., Singapore
Whitehall Books Limited, Wellington, New Zealand

10   9   8   7   6   5   4   3   2   1

Library of Congress Cataloging in Publication Data
Carr, Rachel E.
    Wheel, camel, fish, and plow.
    Includes index.
    SUMMARY: Outlines a mental and physical fitness
program based on the disciplines of yoga. Also
discusses running, diet, and nutrition.
    1. Yoga, Hatha—Juvenile literature.   2. Physical
fitness—Juvenile literature.   [1. Yoga. 2. Physical
fitness. 3. Health]   I. Title.
RA781.7.C369   613.7'046   81-7319
ISBN 0-13-956045-9   AACR2

CONTENTS

ACKNOWLEDGMENTS

I am grateful to the parents who have permitted their children to be photographed for this book and to the children themselves for their desire to become involved in this body-mind fitness program. In alphabetical order, they are: Kariem Amatullah, Gordon Anderson, Leslie Best, Lori Bressman, Mark Browning, Kin Chung Chan, Felicia Davis, Moira Fox, Andrew Gardner, Philippe Genin, Daniel Gross, Matthew Gross, Earl Jarrett, Emma Kuhn, Mark Levine, Kirsten Loft, Sheila Mullen, Jennifer Stewart, Shari Traister, Heidi Untener, Robert Watts. Cover photo: Lori Bressman and Daniel Gross.

My gratitude is also extended to Educational Activities for permission to use some of the photographs from my record album, *Yoga for Young People*, produced by them.

This book would not have been possible without the assistance of my husband, Edward Kimball, who spent endless hours taking the photographs.

AUTHOR'S NOTE

I have purposely chosen a variety of models for the exercises in this book in order to show what people with different bodies are capable of doing. Some people are naturally limber, others are stiff. But everyone can become more limber through a regular practice of these yoga disciplines.

This book is dedicated to all young people who want to achieve fitness of body and mind.

GETTING READY FOR YOGA

This book is designed to build harmony between your body and mind through the disciplines of yoga, an ancient Indian science of physical and mental health.

Yoga exercises are completely different from ordinary calisthenics. In yoga, you use your mind as much as your body. Many exercises resemble the shape of an animal, bird, insect, or object. Center your attention on the image of the cobra; your spine moves in a slow snakelike manner in rhythm with your breathing. In the bow, your limbs become taut as bowstrings. In the locust, your legs lift up swiftly like a locust in flight.

These rhythmic movements will give you a flexible, elastic body with good muscular tone. When you learn to breathe correctly with your diaphragm (the main muscle in breathing), you can increase your energy and calm your nerves.

The mind-sharpening exercises in this book will help you concentrate better. As you learn to sit still with your eyes closed, you will feel an inner calm. This quiet mental state can help you control your anger; you may find new ways to handle your problems.

Exercise is fun if you do not have to rush through it. To get the most out of this yoga program, separate your daily practice into two sessions. Physical exercises and deep breathing are best done in the early morning to limber you up; the mental exercises can be done in the late afternoon.

All you need is a firm exercise mat or a thick towel over a rug; even folded blankets will do. Wear lightweight clothes to give you freedom of movement. Wait at least an hour after you have eaten so the food will be properly digested. Exercise in a quiet, well-ventilated area where the light is soft. Make sure the room is not too warm or too cold for comfort.

Don't be impatient if you are not limber. Through daily practice, your flexibility will increase, and you will begin to reach higher, bend lower, and stretch farther. Remember to breathe quietly and deeply as you move each muscle and stretch each joint. By centering your mind on the posture you are doing, you will feel the spirit as you become one with it.

UNDERSTANDING YOUR BODY

The human body is an engineering marvel of strength, flexibility, and balance. Two hundred and six bones anchor some six hundred muscles. The bones are linked by bands of elastic tissue called ligaments. The ligaments allow the joints such as hips, knees, and shoulders to move freely. These joints are lined with cartilage, a smooth tissue that acts much like the bearings in a machine to reduce friction. In a healthy body the bones, muscles, and connective tissues all function with perfect teamwork.

It is the spine that gives the body its ability to bend and twist. Shaped like a question mark, the spine is a long column of bony rings called vertebrae. Between each pair of vertebrae is a disc that acts as a shock absorber. Strong, flexible back muscles help support the spine and keep the discs from being injured.

The muscles of your body that you can control are called the voluntary muscles. You use them in throwing a ball, running, or exercising. Voluntary muscles work in pairs: one contracts to pull a bone forward, then the other contracts to pull it back. When these muscles are well-toned, they can perform with the speed and power you see in professional athletes, dancers, and gymnasts.

In a body with good posture, the bones and joints are able to take the stress of weight and movement, and the muscular system is firmly balanced to hold the organs in place. Good posture is more than simply standing straight and tall. It involves strong muscles that protect the spine. If you have a tendency to slouch or stand swaybacked, it is an indication that your muscles are weak. The correct way to stand comfortably is with the buttocks tucked in. Simply tightening the muscles of your buttocks now and then will help to improve your posture.

Slumped—poor posture

Good—strong posture

Nature has made no two bodies alike, even though the bone structure and muscular system are the same. Some people are more limber than others; some are physically stronger. As you become aware of your body, you will know what it is capable of doing. You will learn how you can increase your agility and strength through limbering and strengthening exercises.

No two bodies are alike. Some are more flexible than others. Tight-muscled people can increase their flexibility through limbering exercises.

A healthy body working at its peak. When muscles are well-toned, they can perform with agility and power.

THE RIGHT WAY TO BREATHE

Breathing is so natural that most of us do not realize how important it is to breathe properly. It is not the amount of air that matters, but the way the air is used within the body.

Nature intended us to breathe deeply, filling the lungs with air. When we absorb oxygen through the lungs, which are large spongy organs with thin walls, the body tissues are nourished.

Most of the time, we should breathe only through the nose. This is because the air-cleaning process for the lungs begins with the hairs in the nostrils; these act as filters, trapping dust particles that are in the air. When we breathe out (exhale) through the nostrils rather than the mouth, the lungs are strengthened because they take a longer time to deflate. There are exceptions: in brisk walking or in running, we get a quicker supply of oxygen by exhaling through the mouth.

BASIC BREATHING

Practice this breathing exercise lying on your back with knees bent. Place one hand on your abdomen to feel the movement of the diaphragm. This dome-shaped muscle separates the chest from the abdomen. It is the main muscle you use in breathing.

Inhale (breathe in) through the nostrils with mouth closed. You will feel your abdomen expanding. Keep your chest still. Then as you exhale (breathe out) through the nostrils, feel the abdomen contracting.

Practice these movements with your eyes closed. Concentrate on the movement of the abdomen. This type of breathing exercises the diaphragm and stretches the lower portions of the lungs. When you are familiar with this breathing technique, begin to do it rhythmically by counting to yourself. Inhale to the count of five seconds, and exhale to the count of ten seconds. Repeat ten times without stopping. Keep your eyes closed.

The key to correct breathing is simple to remember: Inhale and expand (push out) your abdomen; exhale and contract (pull in) your abdomen.

Think of the flow of your breath into your body as if you were pouring water into a pitcher: first fill the bottom, then the middle, and finally the top. When emptying, the top is first, then the middle, and last the bottom.

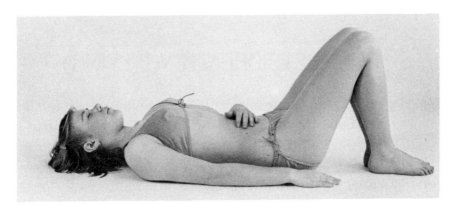

Place one hand on your abdomen to feel the movement as you breathe in and out.

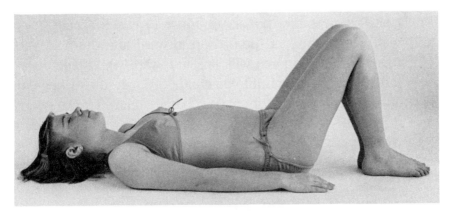

As you inhale through the nostrils (mouth closed), feel the abdomen expanding. Keep your chest still.

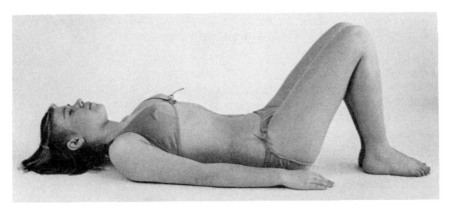

As you exhale through the nostrils (mouth closed), feel the abdomen contracting. Keep your chest still.

COMPLETE BREATHING (LYING)

Once you know how to breathe with your diaphragm, you will find that you can pull the air all the way up into the topmost part of your lungs; then, with the same control, you can let the air out slowly. In this type of complete breathing, you will feel the flow of energy surging through your body as you concentrate on the power of your breath.

Lie on your back with legs outstretched and together, arms to the sides. Inhale deeply (through the nostrils); at the same time, stretch your arms overhead until the backs of your hands are on the floor. The air is now pulled up into your chest. Exhale slowly and raise your arms; let them drop forward and down to your sides again. Your abdomen will sink in toward your spine.

Practice this exercise until you can coordinate the movements of your arms with the rhythm of your breath. Inhale for five counts and exhale for ten counts. Repeat ten times without stopping. Keep your eyes closed.

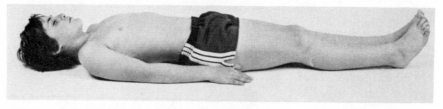

With eyes closed, lie flat with arms at sides.

Inhale deeply. At the same time, stretch your arms overhead until the backs of your hands touch the floor. You will notice that this action pulls in your abdomen as the air is drawn up into the topmost parts of your lungs.

Note: If you feel lightheaded when doing this breathing, stop and rest a moment. This is caused by hyperventilation (too much oxygen absorbed at one time). With practice, you will become accustomed to deep breathing.

COMPLETE BREATHING (STANDING)

Stand with your legs together, arms at your sides. Inhale deeply; at the same time raise your arms overhead. Interlock the fingers of both hands. Stretch fully, rising on tiptoe, while holding your breath. Exhale, let your heels down; bend forward and down to touch your toes, or as far as you can reach without straining. Inhale, stretch upward again; exhale and lower your arms to the sides. Repeat ten times without stopping. Keep your eyes closed.

This is a quick way to pick up energy and keep your mind alert.

ABDOMINAL LIFT

This exercise must never be done on a full stomach. Wait at least two hours after a meal to avoid nausea.

Stand with legs apart, hands on your thighs. Bend slightly forward. Exhale vigorously through your mouth, making a "ha" sound. This will create a vacuum, caving the abdomen in. *Without inhaling* (important and not easy to do at first), forcibly pull in the abdominal muscles by drawing them up toward the spine, pressing against the rib cage. Hold for ten counts *without breathing.* Relax. Take a deep breath, exhale, and repeat ten times.

Benefits: Works wonders on soft abdominal muscles.

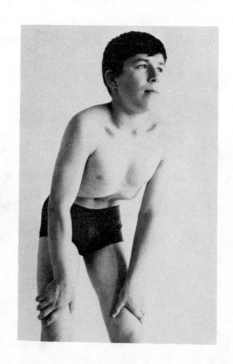

MIND CONTROL

MIND-SHARPENING EXERCISES

These mind-sharpening exercises will heighten your power of observation and focus your concentration. Each one should be practiced separately for a week, about five minutes each day. To keep your mind free, sit in a quiet place with no distractions or music.

CONCENTRATE ON AN OBJECT

You can choose any object for this exercise. Look for something with color, shape, and texture: a flower, for instance, or a smooth, sturdy vase.

24

This is the way to practice concentrating on an object, such as a rose. Begin to study the different textures and colors of the flower. Notice how the leaves grow and how the petals embrace one another. Concentrate on every part of the flower until you have absorbed it, even inhaling its fragrance. Then close your eyes. In your mind's eye, recall the color of the rose, its shape, its texture, and its fragrance. If your mind begins to stray, coax it back gently; never force it. If you can't keep the image in your mind, open your eyes and gaze at the rose again. Then close your eyes and repeat the same mental exercise until you can see the flower down to its smallest detail in your mind's eye.

After you have spent a week on this mind-sharpening exercise, you will find that your concentration has become strong and sharp. You can focus your mind more easily. You will also be able to read for longer periods of time and remember what you have read without struggling.

CONCENTRATE ON NUMBERS

In this mind-sharpening exercise, you will need ten 5 x 7 cards. Write one number (from 1 to 10) on each card in thick black strokes. Put the numbers in order and place the cards in a pile in front of you.

Begin with number 1. Inhale deeply and concentrate on this number. Focus your entire attention on the card. Then close your eyes and visualize that number in your mind's eye. Open your eyes. Turn to number 2 and repeat the same mental exercise until you have reached the number 10. Then reverse the numbers. Start with 10 and go down to 1 in the same way.

As your power of concentration develops, you will be able to visualize the numbers without actually looking at them. Start by

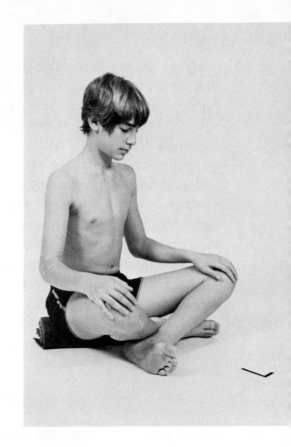

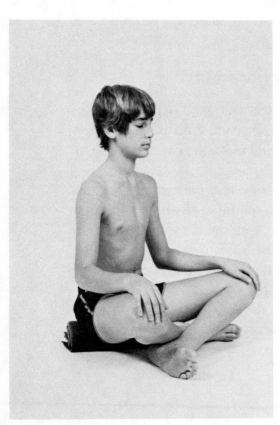

26

breathing quietly for a few seconds to still your mind and keep it from wandering. Then inhale deeply and outline the number 1 in your mind's eye. Erase it mentally as you exhale. Inhale again and outline the number 2. Repeat until you have reached the number 10. Then begin to count down, going from 10 to 1. If your mind strays during this exercise, coax it back gently to the numbers.

Practice this exercise for a week. You will find that your mind is able to concentrate more easily on the mental images of the numbers. Your ability to do this will heighten your powers of concentration in other ways as well.

CONCENTRATE ON A CANDLE FLAME

This mental exercise is done in a dark room so the candle flame will not lose its luminous quality. Gazing steadily at the flame for seconds at a time stimulates the nerve centers in your brain; your mind can concentrate more easily on a single image, first by looking at it, then by seeing it in your mind's eye.

Place the candle at easy viewing distance and gaze at the flame until your eyes begin to water. This takes from 20 to 30 seconds, depending on how sensitive your eyes are to light. Then put the candle out and close your eyes. You will see the glow of the flame in your mind's eye. Hold on to this image. Interesting things begin to happen. First the flame will appear bright. Then it will take different shapes and different degrees of brightness. It will grow longer and move into the distance. A black halo with a dotted flame in the center will appear and gradually disappear. When you are no longer able to hold the image, light the candle and concentrate on its flame again.

Repeat this mental exercise a few minutes a day for a week. You will be amazed at how quickly your powers of concentration will improve. Each day you will be able to hold the flame longer in your mind's eye; your ability to observe will also improve. You will have a strong mental image of the candle's texture and the intensity of its orange-colored flame. The flame itself has a remarkably calming influence on the mind.

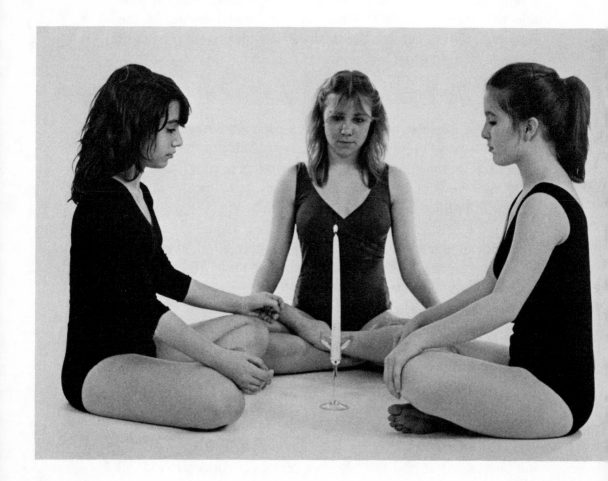

MEDITATION

This is a very important mental exercise for daily meditation. It will help you become a more understanding and considerate person.

   Sit in a quiet place where you will not be disturbed. Begin to relax your mind by breathing quietly and deeply with your eyes closed. Concentrate on the rhythm of your breath. Feel it rising and falling as you inhale and exhale smoothly through your nostrils. While listening to your breath, turn your mind inward. Meditate on the following five principles that lead to higher thinking.

1. Silence: When you are silent, you will still your mind.

2. Listening: When you listen, you learn.

3. Remembering: When you remember, you become more considerate of others.

4. Understanding: When you understand, your actions will have more meaning.

5. Acting: Finally, when you act, it should be with a gentle heart and an understanding mind. Only then can you truly say that you are able to forgive those who have harmed you, and that you are a better person for it.

LIMBERING

These limbering exercises are important if you are tight-muscled or in poor physical shape. Do them slowly so you can feel each stretch of a muscle and loosening of a joint.

KNEE STRETCH

Sit on a small cushion so your body will be slightly raised. Stretch your legs out. Bend your right knee and bring your right foot over your left thigh. Press down gently on the bent knee, but don't force it down farther than it can go. Hold for ten counts to feel the stretch. Straighten the leg. Bounce it up and down to stimulate circulation. Repeat ten times, alternating right and left leg.

Benefits: Limbers tight leg muscles and increases their range of motion.

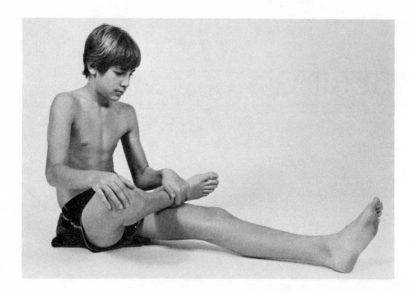

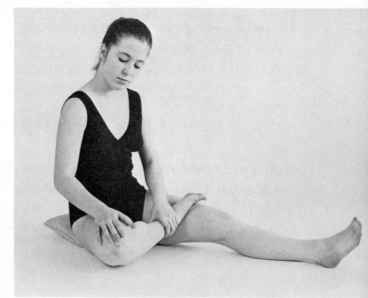

In the knee stretch, some people can press the bent knee closer to the ground than others.

HEAD-TO-KNEE STRETCH

Lie on your back with knees bent to your chest. Interlock your fingers around your knees. Keep your eyes closed. Inhale while raising your head to touch the knees. Exhale. Hold for five counts. Lower the legs and head. Repeat ten times.

Benefits: Relieves pain in the lower back; limbers stiff spine; strengthens weak back muscles.

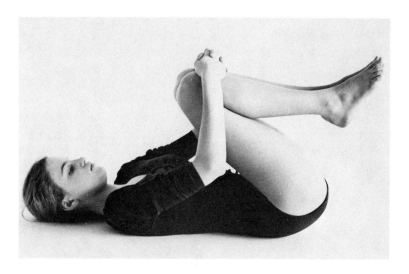

SIDE STRETCHES

1. Lie on your left side; left elbow is bent with hand supporting your head. Inhale and raise your right leg. Grasp the foot with your right hand. Hold for ten counts. Exhale. Lower your leg. Repeat five times.

2. With right hand in front for balance, inhale and raise both legs together. Hold for ten counts. Exhale. Lower legs. Repeat five times.

3. With right hand in front for balance, inhale and bend knees toward your chest. Without letting them touch the floor, straighten your legs, then bend them again toward the chest. Breathe freely and repeat ten times without stopping.

4. Turn and lie on your right side. Repeat the sequence of side stretches.

Benefits: Tones waistline, hips, and thighs; limbers knees; improves balance.

BACK STRETCH

Stand with your back straight. Cross your right arm behind your back; the back of your hand should touch your spine, with fingers pointing upward. Raise your left arm over your left shoulder. Grasp the fingers of your right hand. Hold for five counts while breathing freely. Repeat six times, alternating right and left arms.

If you are unable to do this stretch, use a handkerchief or scarf. Grasp it at both ends. Try to bring your hands closer together each time to increase the stretch.

Benefits: Improves posture; limbers shoulder muscles.

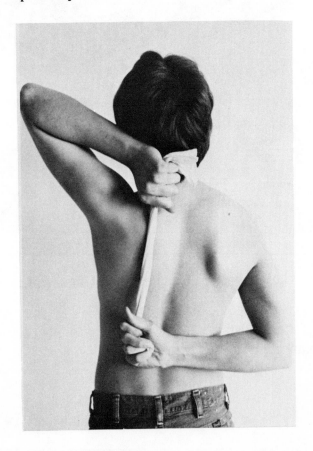

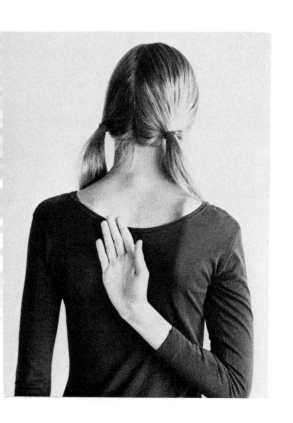

HEAD ROLL

Keep your eyes closed and let your neck rotate loosely in a circular motion: forward and down, right, back, left, and forward. Repeat five times while breathing freely. Reverse direction and repeat five times.

This exercise can be done anywhere.

Benefits: Releases built-up tension in back of neck and shoulders; limbers tight muscles.

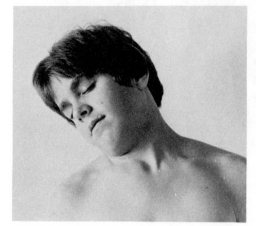
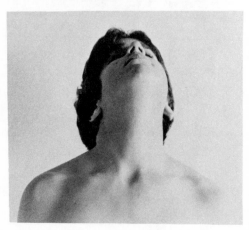
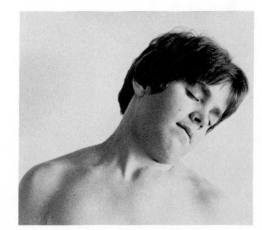

YOGA POSTURES

The thirteen basic yoga postures given in this section resemble the shapes of animals, birds, insects, and objects. (Exceptions are the Salute to the Sun and the Headstand.) These body shapes let you use your imagination as you try to become one with each posture you are doing. Try to feel the rhythmic movements, which require strong, flexible muscles.

To get the most out of these creative postures, do each one slowly. Breathe rhythmically while holding the pose for a few seconds to feel the complete stretch. The more controlled you are in doing the movements, the more benefit you will gain from these creative body shapes.

COBRA

1. Lie face down. Bend your elbows, keeping your hands close to your shoulders with palms down. Keep feet together.

2. Inhale while slowly raising your chest until your arms are fully stretched. Arch your neck and look up. Hold for ten counts while breathing freely.

3. Slowly lower your body until your forehead touches the floor. Repeat five times. Movements should be snakelike and slow.

Benefits: Increases spinal stretch; strengthens lower back.

LOCUST

1. Lie face down, chin on the floor. Keep your legs together and your eyes closed. Clench your fists and place them, with thumbs touching, under your groin.

2. Inhale. Press your fists against the floor, using them to help as you thrust your legs up. Keep your head down. Hold for ten counts while breathing freely. Lower legs. Repeat five times.

Benefits: Strengthens weak back muscles; tones abdomen and legs.

BOW

1. Lie face down, with knees bent, hands holding on to your ankles or feet.

2. Inhale and stretch upward; your arms are fully stretched and pulling on your ankles. Breathe freely. Keep your head up while holding your body taut for ten counts. Repeat five times.

3. When your muscles are strong enough, rock back and forth ten times.

Benefits: Tones muscles in arms, legs, abdomen, and spine.

COBRA–LOCUST–BOW

You can combine the Cobra, Locust, and Bow into a series of smooth, flowing movements.

SHOULDERSTAND

1. Lie on your back, arms at your sides, palms down. Close your eyes. Inhale and raise your legs, keeping knees straight.

2. Continue to raise your legs until they are over your head.

3. Place your hands against your waist; raise your legs straight up to a vertical position. The weight of your body should be on your shoulders and arms, with your chin pressing against your chest. Keep legs relaxed but straight, toes pointing up. You should not feel any strain. Adjust your neck until it feels comfortable. Hold for 20 counts to feel the blood supply close to the skin in the face and neck. (Have someone check the position of your body. Toes should be directly over the head, not beyond it.)

4. Bend your left knee, with the sole of your foot touching the right knee. Hold for ten counts. Straighten the leg to a vertical position. Repeat with the right leg.

5. Bring both legs over your head. Balance your body with hands resting on the knees. Hold for ten counts.

6. To come down, place your hands on the mat, as in Step 1, and gradually lower your legs. Arch your neck; your head will remain on the mat as your legs are lowered. Repeat five times.

Benefits: Tones the entire body.

PLOW

If these stretches are difficult for you, practice them gradually to increase flexibility in your spine.

1. Lie on your back, with arms at your sides and legs together. Close your eyes. Inhale and raise legs overhead, pressing down with the palms of your hands.

2. Exhale. Lower your legs as far back as you can without straining. Hold for ten counts, breathing freely; feel the stretch along your spine and in your hamstrings (the tendons at the back of your knees). Inhale; return your legs forward and down to the floor. To keep your head on the floor, arch your neck back when lowering

your legs. Repeat five times slowly. Try to stretch a little farther each time. With practice, your toes will eventually touch the floor.

3. (You can do this step when your spine has become more flexible.) Inhale; stretch your arms overhead and raise your legs, arching your spine.

4. Exhale. Lower your legs as far back as you can. Hold for ten counts; breathe freely, feel the stretch. Inhale; return your legs forward and down. Exhale; raise arms and bring them down to your sides. Repeat five times slowly. Try to stretch a little farther each time.

Benefits: Limbers spine; tones arms and legs; stretches hamstrings.

FISH

1. Lie on your back, with hands under your buttocks, palms down. Keep legs together and eyes closed.

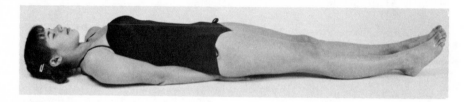

2. Inhale; arch your spine to create a bridge between your head and buttocks. Breathe freely while holding for ten counts.

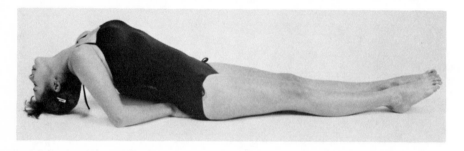

3. Slip hands out from under your body and place them on your chest, palms touching. Concentrate on the image of a fish while holding for ten counts. Lower your spine. Repeat five times.

Benefits: Excellent toning and limbering for the spine, neck, and lower back. Mind is calm while resting in this pose.

CAMEL

1. Kneel with your legs slightly apart and your hands on your waist. Inhale; bend back, arching your spine. Grasp your ankles or heels. Keep your neck relaxed. Hold for ten counts while breathing freely. Return to kneeling position. Repeat five times.

2. Arch your spine in the kneeling position. Place your palms together below the chest. Hold for ten counts while breathing freely. Return to kneeling position. Repeat five times.

Benefits: Develops flexible spine; limbers knees; firms hips and thighs as muscles are lengthened and toned.

WHEEL

To do this exercise well, your arms and legs must be strong and your spine limber. It takes practice.

1. Lie on your back, with your knees bent and your feet drawn close to your buttocks. Bend your elbows and place your hands beside your shoulders, with palms down.

2. Inhale while raising your body off the mat. Press down on your hands and feet to arch your spine.

3. Raise yourself higher, straightening your arms. Hold for ten counts while breathing freely. Lower your body slowly. Repeat five times.

4. When your muscles are stronger, bend your right leg so the foot rests on your left knee. Lower the leg and repeat with the left leg.

5. Raise your right leg straight up, keeping your left foot and your hands firmly on the floor. Lower the leg and repeat with the left leg.

6. To come down, reverse the first three steps until your body is lowered. Repeat three times.

Benefits: Strengthens arms, legs, and spine.

TREE

To steady your balance, concentrate on an object at eye level.

1. Stand firmly on your left leg. Bend your right leg and bring your right foot up over the left thigh, sole facing up. Grasp your foot and ankle with both hands.

2. Press the foot against your thigh. Inhale; slowly raise your arms overhead with fingertips touching. Breathe freely while concentrating on the image of a tree. Hold for ten counts.

Benefits: Limbers knees and stretches muscles in arms and spine. This is an exercise for balance, posture, and concentration.

ARROW

To steady your balance, concentrate on an object at eye level.

1. Stand on your left leg. Bend your right knee and grasp your right foot with your right hand. Inhale while raising your left arm, stretching it up. Hold for ten counts while breathing freely.

2. Bend forward and stretch your right leg and arm back, away from your body. Lower your left arm to form a straight line with the right arm. When arms are on the same plane, hold for ten counts. Concentrate on the image of an arrow. Repeat six times, alternating left and right legs.

Benefits: Entire body is stretched, toned, and firmed. This is an exercise for balance, posture, and concentration.

CROW

1. Squat with your knees apart, elbows close inside your knees, palms down on the floor. Rest on your toes.

2. Inhale while pressing down on your hands; at the same time raise your legs off the floor and rest your knees on your elbows. (This may take some practice if your wrists are weak.) When your balance is secure, hold for ten counts, breathing freely.

Benefits: Improves balance; strengthens arms and legs.

Balancing in the Crow posture takes practice.

SALUTE TO THE SUN

The twelve movements of this exercise flow into each other, stretching all your muscles to increase their flexibility. It is an excellent warm-up for early morning exercises.

Look through the twelve steps of the exercise to see the sequence of movements. Then try them slowly one at a time, following the photographs.

In looking at the sequence, you will notice that Steps 2 and 3 are repeated in reverse in Steps 10 and 11. In Step 4 the left leg is forward, while in Step 9, the right leg is forward. It takes practice to keep your palms in the same position without shifting them as you move from one step to the next.

Repeat Salute to the Sun six times, slowly and smoothly. In the first sequence of movements, move the right leg back in Step 4 and the left leg back in Step 9. In the second sequence of movements, move the left leg back in Step 4 and the right leg back in Step 9. Keep alternating with each sequence.

1. Stand with legs together, hands close to the chest, with palms touching.

2. Inhale while raising arms overhead. Bend back, arching the spine.

3. Exhale while bending forward until hands touch the floor. They should be in line with the feet.

4. Inhale while moving right foot backward until the knee touches the floor. Keep left foot firmly on the floor.

5. Hold your breath. Without shifting the right leg, raise the knee off the floor; then move the left foot back next to the right foot. Toes are turned in and your body is on a slant, supported by the hands and toes. Look straight ahead.

6. Exhale and lower your body so your forehead and chest touch the floor.

7. Inhale while lowering your buttocks and arching your back. Arms are almost straight, palms still on the floor.

8. Exhale while lifting your back in a cat's stretch. Keep your head between your arms. Don't tense your neck.

9. Inhale while bringing your right foot forward alongside your hands. Toes of left foot and left knee touch the floor.

10. Exhale while bringing the left foot alongside the right and straightening the knees. Hands are in line with the feet. Bring your head close to your knees.

11. Inhale while raising your arms overhead. Bend back, arching your spine.

12. Exhale while returning your arms forward and down to the sides of your body.

HEADSTAND

Most people can learn to stand on their heads safely. But there is a word of caution. If you are overweight or have physical problems, ask your doctor's advice before standing on your head.

The yogis call the headstand the "restorer" of health. When the head is lowered, more blood is sent to the brain. Every part of the body is in control to maintain perfect balance.

THE FIRST STEPS

1. Use a mat or thick folded towel close to a wall for safety. Kneel with legs together, arms in front. Rest your elbows on the mat so that the fingertips of one hand will touch the elbows of the opposite arm.

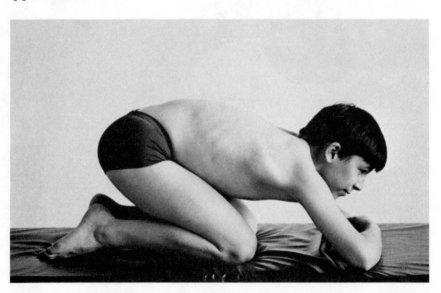

2. Without moving your elbows, stretch arms forward so that your fingers can interlock. This is the correct distance.

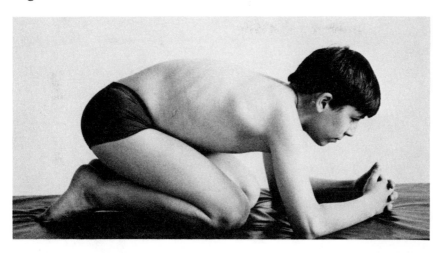

3. Bend so that the top of your head rests on the mat. Your clasped hands encircle your head. Make sure your neck and head feel comfortable. Find the point of balance by adjusting yourself.

4. Raise your buttocks, straighten your legs, and rest on your toes. Then raise and lower your heels to stretch the hamstrings. Repeat ten times.

5. To strengthen your legs, walk in toward your body and away again. Repeat ten times.

COMING UP TO BALANCE

1. Keep your head and arms in position. With help, lift your legs, keeping the knees bent.

2. Bring your feet closer to your buttocks.

3. Raise your legs slowly, keeping your knees bent and your feet above your buttocks.

4. Slowly straighten your legs vertically.

5. When your legs are straight, your toes should be directly above your head, with your buttocks tucked in.

Congratulations! You have completed the thirteen basic yoga postures. Continue to practice each one, using your imagination to become one with each body shape. In the fish pose, for example, a bridge is created between your head and buttocks as you become a floating fish. When you breathe deeply in this tranquil pose, your mind becomes calm. In the tree pose, feel the steadiness of your balance. Your legs are the roots of the tree, and your body is the trunk. Your fingertips, as your arms stretch upward, suggest the leafy tips of the branches.

Work on the exercises that are still difficult for you so that you can increase your flexibility and strength and keep your body well-toned. The combination of postures suggested on page 43 will help you vary your daily practice.

RUNNING

Running is a natural form of exercise. It keeps all the muscles in tone, speeds up the circulation of the blood, helps the digestive system, strengthens the lungs and heart, and is a good way to keep trim.

You can get the full benefit of this exhilarating sport if you run with a natural sense of movement and ease, coordinating your arms and legs with the rhythm of your breath. As you inhale through your nostrils, take three or four steps; then as you exhale through your mouth (for a quicker supply of oxygen), take the same number of steps. After some practice you will begin to feel your own inner rhythm and it will dictate the right pace for you.

Keep your elbows bent but not held rigidly against your chest. Your hands should be relaxed, fingers loosely cupped. Toes should point straight ahead. The forward swing of your leg, which involves the hip, knee, and heel, ends with the heel striking down first. The weight shifts to the ball of your foot and rolls onto the toes. Those who are flat-footed should practice the foot movements slowly to achieve the right rhythm. Let your arms swing freely and comfortably, bringing all muscles into play.

Take it easy when you begin running. Build up your stamina slowly. For the first week run about a mile, or even less. As your breathing rhythm feels easier, increase your distance gradually. Running should always be fun; never tire yourself to the point of

The heel strikes down first. The weight shifts to the ball of the foot and rolls onto the toes.

exhaustion. When you get into the spirit of running, you will begin to enjoy that marvelous sensation of well-being as your lungs take in fresh oxygen and your muscles are exercised from head to toe.

WHAT TO WEAR

Run in loose comfortable clothes: warm in winter, cool in summer. Tightfitting clothing will limit your freedom of movement and cut down the flow of blood to your fingers and toes. Sweat pants and shirts should be worn only in extreme cold. A light waterproof jacket will protect your chest and back, and a woolen cap will absorb perspiration from your head, keeping it warm. Good running shoes with firm soles and arch supports are essential. Thick, soft socks that fit well will absorb perspiration and protect your feet from blisters.

WHERE TO RUN

The ideal places to run are tracks, grass playing fields, or parks. Cement and asphalt are hard on the feet, since each foot hits the ground about 800 times a mile!

WARM-UP EXERCISES

The exercises on pages 76-83 are warm-ups to stretch your muscles and prevent sudden contraction when you are running. This can be both painful and harmful.

STRETCHING ACHILLES TENDON

Lean forward while holding onto a post or wall. Bend your right knee, keeping the sole of your foot flat. Stretch your left leg back, pressing down with your foot. Breathe freely while holding for ten counts; feel the stretch in the Achilles tendon (it joins calf muscles to the heel bone). Repeat six times, alternating right and left legs.

LIMBERING KNEES

Hold onto a post or wall. Bend your right leg up and grasp your ankle with your right hand. Breathe freely while holding for ten counts; feel the stretch in your bent knee as you press your foot close to your buttock. Repeat six times, alternating left and right legs.

WAIST BEND

Stand with your legs apart. Bend to your left while raising your right arm overhead. Your left arm should be down, hand touching your knee. Breathe freely while holding for five counts. Repeat six times, alternating right and left sides.

LEG TWIST

Cross your right foot over your left. Bend to touch your feet, keeping your knees as straight as possible. Breathe freely while holding for five counts. Repeat six times, alternating right and left legs. Do this exercise slowly and gently; don't force it.

HEAD-TO-KNEE BEND

Stand with your legs apart, hands behind your back with fingers interlocked. Inhale while bending forward to touch your right knee with your forehead, or as far as you can reach. Stretch arms upward behind you. Bend your knee a little to increase the stretch. Breathe freely while holding for ten counts. Repeat six times, alternating right and left legs.

FORWARD BEND

Stand with your legs together and arms at your sides. Inhale while bending your left knee forward and sliding your right foot back. Stretch your arms out in front. Breathe freely while holding for five counts to increase your balance and feel the stretch. Repeat six times, alternating left and right legs.

BODY TWIST

Stand with your legs apart. Interlock your fingers in front of you. With one continuous breath, swing your arms around your body: forward and down, to the right, up to the right, back over your head, to the left, and down. Exhale. Repeat five times. Reverse direction and repeat five more times.

Set a modest goal for yourself. Remember that endurance in running is built up gradually. If you overexert yourself, you can injure your knees and feet. Running is an energetic sport and requires caution. Here is a checklist:

1. Wear good running shoes.
2. Wear the right type of clothes in cold weather and in hot weather.
3. Do warm-up exercises.
4. Before running, particularly in hot weather, drink six to eight ounces of water to replenish the body fluid you will lose through perspiration.
5. Cool off slowly after running.

If running is too strenuous for you, try race-walking. Step by step, day by day, you will begin to feel more energetic physically and more alert mentally.

EATING RIGHT

What you eat affects the way you grow and develop. Your body works twenty-four hours a day, always building itself up, repairing itself, and discarding waste products. It needs a constant supply of nutrients to help the organs, nerves, and muscles function properly.

Most nutrition experts agree that there is no single pattern of diet that must be followed for good health. A well-balanced diet with emphasis on fresh fruits and vegetables will provide everything you need: proteins, carbohydrates, fats, vitamins, and minerals.

PROTEINS are found in meat, poultry, fish, milk, cheese, and eggs. Bread and cereal are also sources of protein. So are such vegetables as soybeans, dried beans, and peanuts. Proteins are the building blocks of every cell in the body.

CARBOHYDRATES are the major source of energy. They are found in cereal grains, fruits, and vegetables, as well as in sugar and honey.

FATS exist in butter, margarine, shortening, vegetable oils, nuts, dairy products, and fatty meats. Fats provide energy and help to carry certain vitamins throughout the body. However, too much fat can lead to overweight, which may cause medical problems later on.

VITAMINS are important. Though they don't directly create energy or build tissues, vitamins are involved in the release of energy within the body and in the process of tissue building. Some vitamins control the ways the body handles food. Vitamins are found in many natural foods, such as fruits, vegetables, grain products, meats, and dairy products.

MINERALS are also necessary for the body to function properly. Calcium, found in milk and green leafy vegetables, and iron, found in liver, raisins, and whole-grain bread, are two important minerals. Eating a wide variety of natural foods will provide all the necessary minerals for a healthy body.

The body uses food to build new cells and to create energy to do the things you want to do. So it is important to replace the supply of each kind of nutrient every day.

The list of important foods and liquids given below has been tested and proven to have all the known elements of nutrition required for a daily diet.

BE SURE TO HAVE EVERY DAY:

MILK: 1 or 2 glasses

MEAT, FISH, POULTRY, CHEESE, EGGS, DRIED BEANS, PEAS, OR LENTILS: 1 or 2 servings.

BREAD OR CEREAL: 1 or 2 servings of whole-grain or enriched. One-half cup cereal equals 1 slice of bread.

HIGH VITAMIN C FRUIT (fresh, whenever possible): 1 serving at least of
>
> orange or orange juice
> grapefruit or grapefruit juice
> tomato or tomato juice
> cantaloupe or strawberries

OTHER FRESH FRUITS: 1 or 2 servings

VEGETABLES: 2 servings (raw or lightly cooked);
>
> 1 serving of dark green leafy vegetables,
> such as broccoli, spinach, escarole, or
> 1 serving of deep yellow vegetables, such as carrots,
> sweet potatoes, or squash, plus 1 other vegetable.

(Menus based on information from U.S. Department of Health, Bureau of Nutrition.)

Refer to this checklist whenever you need a snack in between meals. These foods are high in nutrition and will help you develop the habit of eating right.

HIGH-NUTRITION SNACKS:

dried and fresh fruits
raw and cooked vegetables
fruit and vegetable juices (unsweetened)
low-sugar dry cereals and milk
yogurt
cheese slices
nuts

As much as possible, avoid foods like these that are high in calories and low in nutrition.

HIGH-CALORIE, LOW-NUTRITION SNACKS:

sugar	chocolates
soft drinks	cakes
syrups	pastries
jellies	sugared doughnuts
jams	most cookies
sweetened juices	potato chips
candy	pretzels

HELPFUL TIPS FOR EATING RIGHT

Don't Skip Breakfast Nutritionally, this is the most important meal of the day. After twelve hours or more without eating, your body needs food for energy. A good breakfast makes you more alert and less tired during the day. There are certain foods you can eat to awaken your digestive process, such as fresh strawberries with a glass of milk or cereal. Choose a high-nutrition cooked or packaged cereal.

Cut Down on Sugar   Sugary snack foods provide little nutrition. They are low in the vitamins and other nutrients your body needs. When you fill up on junk food, you aren't hungry for the nutritious foods you need for good health. Too much sugar is also an important factor in overweight and in tooth decay. Train your taste buds to eat food without added sugar. You will be surprised at how sweet fruits such as strawberries, cantaloupe, and even grapefruit will taste. Vegetables too, such as carrots and tomatoes, have a naturally sweet flavor.

Keep Your Weight Down   Bad eating habits (too many starches and sweets) and too little exercise are usually the reasons for weight gain. But crash diets are not the answer. You will probably lose those extra pounds while you're on the crash diet, but when you go back to your "normal" way of eating that caused you to gain weight, the pounds will soon return. To lose weight, eating habits must be changed. A daily program of physical exercise and a well-balanced diet will keep your weight down and your body running smoothly.

Don't Be a Compulsive Eater   Some people eat more when they feel depressed or tired. You may be "addicted" to a particular food. Potato chips and peanuts are examples of so-called "food addictions." The person addicted to them is unable to stop until the entire package is eaten! The best solution is to eliminate that food from your diet until the compulsive eating habit has disappeared. This takes willpower.

Don't Eat Too Fast   Never eat on the run and gulp down your food. You won't digest it properly and you tend to consume more calories than you realize. When you eat too fast, your body mechanism does not have time to tell you that you have eaten enough; it takes about twenty minutes for this to happen. Eating slowly means you will eat less and enjoy it more.

Advice from a Specialist   "Eating right is the only answer," says Dr. John Beaty, a specialist in nutrition. "Vegetables, for instance, should never be overcooked because they lose their vitamin-mineral content. As much as possible, eat raw fruit and under-cooked vegetables. Avoid sugar and fatty foods, starches, soft drinks that contain carbohydrates....Most important, enjoy your meals whenever you can in quiet surroundings where there is no disturbing conversation or stress."

CHARTS FOR A DAILY FITNESS PROGRAM

This chart will help you plan your daily exercise routine and meditation. You may want to separate the two programs. For example, do all the physical exercises at one time in the early morning. The oxygen you inhale will make you more alert, particularly if you find it difficult to wake up early. In the late afternoon, do the mind-control exercises. They will calm you after a long day at school. At the same time, your power of concentration will be increased for any work you must do.

You can make exercise a pleasurable daily habit. Once you succeed, it will become an important part of your life.

PHYSICAL PROGRAM
20 minutes a day

BREATHING

Basic Breathing
(pp. 18-19)

**Complete Breathing
(lying and standing)**
(pp. 20-21)

Abdominal Lift
(p. 22)

LIMBERING

Knee Stretch
(pp. 31-32)

Head-to-Knee Stretch
(p. 33)

Side Stretches
(pp. 34-35)

Back Stretch
(pp. 36-37)

Head Roll
(p. 38)

13 YOGA POSTURES

Cobra
(p. 40)

Locust
(p. 41)

Bow
(p. 42)

Shoulderstand
(pp. 43-45)

Plow
(pp. 46-47)

Fish
(pp. 48-49)

Camel
(pp. 49-50)

Wheel
(pp. 51-53)

Tree
(pp. 54-55)

Arrow
(pp. 56-57)

Crow
(pp. 58-59)

Salute to the Sun
(pp. 59-65)

Headstand
(pp. 66-71)

MIND CONTROL PROGRAM
10 minutes a day

Do any one of these mind-sharpening exercises each day: Concentrate on an Object (pp. 23-25); Concentrate on Numbers (pp. 25-27); Concentrate on a Candle Flame (pp. 27-28).

Spend about five minutes each day on mediation. As guidelines, meditate on the principles of higher thinking on page 30.